pilgrim

TURNING TO CHRIST
A COURSE FOR THE CHRISTIAN JOURNEY

Church Publishing
NEW YORK

Authors and Contributors

Authors

Stephen Cottrell is the Bishop of Chelmsford
Steven Croft is the Bishop of Sheffield
Paula Gooder is a leading New Testament writer and lecturer
Robert Atwell is the Bishop of Stockport
Sharon Ely Pearson is a Christian educator in The Episcopal Church

Contributors

Nick Baines is the Bishop of Bradford
Stephen Conway is the Bishop of Ely

pilgrim

TURNING TO CHRIST
A COURSE FOR THE CHRISTIAN JOURNEY

STEPHEN COTTRELL
STEVEN CROFT
PAULA GOODER
ROBERT ATWELL
SHARON ELY PEARSON

Contributions from
NICK BAINES
STEPHEN CONWAY

Church Publishing
NEW YORK

First published in the United Kingdom in 2013 by

Church House Publishing
Church House
Great Smith Street
London SW1P 3AZ

Original material written for the U.S. version © 2016
Sharon Ely Pearson

First published in the United States in 2016 by

Church Publishing, Incorporated.
19 East 34th Street
New York, New York 10016
www.churchpublishing.org

Cover and contents design by David McNeill, Revo Design.

Library of Congress Cataloging-in-Publication Data

A record of this book is available from the Library of Congress.

ISBN-13: 978-0-89869-938-8 (pbk.)
ISBN-13: 978-0-89869-939-5 (ebook)

Printed in the United States of America

CONTENTS

WELCOME TO *PILGRIM*

Welcome to this course of exploration into the truth of the Christian faith as it has been revealed in Jesus Christ and lived out in his Church down through the centuries.

The aim of this course is to help people explore what it means to become disciples of Jesus Christ. From the very beginning of his ministry, Jesus called people to follow him and become his disciples. The Church in every generation shares in the task of helping others hear Christ's call to them and follow him.

We hope the course will help you to understand this faith and to see how it can be lived out each day, and that it will equip you to make a decision about whether to be part of this Church. This will either happen by being baptized and confirmed, if this has not happened to you before, or by a renewal of baptismal vows.

You won't be able to find out everything about the Christian faith in any one course. But through the *Pilgrim* course material you will be able to reflect on some of the great texts that have been particularly significant to Christian people from the earliest days of the Church:

- The Creeds
- The Lord's Prayer
- The Beatitudes
- The Commandments

There is one book based on each of these texts in the "Follow" stage of *Pilgrim* (designed for absolute beginners) and one that goes further in the "Grow" (discipleship) stage.

By learning these texts, reflecting upon them, and seeing what they mean for your life, you will make a journey through the great story of the Christian faith. And you will do this in the company of a small group of fellow travelers: people like you who want to find out more about the Christian faith and are considering its claims and challenges.

In other words, this course is for people who are *not yet Christians* but who are open to finding out more and *for those who are just beginning the journey*. People who want some sort of *refresher course* are also very welcome. In walking with you on this journey we are not assuming that you necessarily share the beliefs that are being explored, just that you want to find out about them.

This course will approach the great issues of faith not by trying to persuade you to believe, but by encouraging you to practice the ancient disciplines of biblical reflection and prayer which have always been at the heart of the living out of Christian faith.

We don't think these are things that should only be practiced once you have come to faith. Rather, they can be the means by which faith is received and then strengthened within us.

Each book has six or seven sessions, and in each session you will find:

- a **theme**
- some **opening prayers**
- a **"conversation-starter"**
- an opportunity to **reflect** on a **reading** from Scripture (the Bible)
- a short **article** from a contemporary Christian writer on the theme
- some **questions** to address
- a further time of **prayer**
- finally, a **"sending out"** section, with suggestions for further reflection and selected quotations from the great tradition of Christian writing to help you do so.

This pattern of contemplation and discussion will, we believe, help you to decide whether you wish to respond to Christ and be part of his Church. Remember that the Church is not a group of men and women who are, themselves, certain about all these things, but who "believe, with God's help" (this is what you are asked at baptism) and then go on following Jesus Christ and continuing the journey of faith.

We all learn in different ways, and there is a variety of material here to support you. Different people will receive something from the different parts of the session according to their own learning style.

At the end of this course, we hope you will have made some new friends and explored quite a lot of areas of Christian faith. Just as importantly, you will have been given confidence to read the Bible prayerfully and critically, and you will have, if you wish, established a pattern for prayer. We hope that *Pilgrim* will help you lay a foundation for a lifetime of learning more about God's love revealed in Jesus Christ and what it means to be his disciple.

This little book gives you all you need to begin this great journey. You are standing where millions of men and women have stood: you have caught a glimpse of who God is, and you are puzzled and curious to know whether the claims of the Christian faith can be trusted and whether they actually make any difference to life.

This book and this course can help you. You will need the book for each session, but outside of the sessions you may want to look each week at the material you are about to study together. As the course goes on, you may want to take time each week to look back at what you have already covered as you move forward on your own pilgrimage.

INTRODUCTION TO *TURNING TO CHRIST*

The seven sessions in this book explore the questions candidates are asked when they become a follower of Jesus, the beginning of the pilgrim way. If you decide that you want to follow Jesus and become a Christian, then if you haven't already been baptized that is what will happen. Baptism is a public service of commitment to follow Jesus and be part of his Church. You are washed with water as a sign of your sharing in the death and resurrection of Jesus.

If you have been baptized then you will probably be confirmed. This is the service where you own for yourselves promises that were made on your behalf by others. If you have already been baptized and confirmed, then there is still an opportunity to reaffirm your Christian faith, and again the same questions are asked. They go back a very long way. In most respects, the questions that candidates are asked today are the same questions new Christians were asked in the earliest days of the Church.

They fall into two parts. The first set of questions is known as "The Renunciations and Adhesions" (affirmations). The questions are directed to the heart. Some of the language can be a little daunting. We don't always use language about "the devil" and "evil" in everyday life. Don't be worried about this. Some of it will be explored in the sessions.

The Church uses bold language to speak about the reality of sin and evil and the hope of Christ. But the heart of these questions is very simple: it is about which way we are facing and who we are following. So we are invited to turn away from sin, darkness, and evil, and turn towards Christ. He is the one we are invited to follow.

The journey of the Christian faith is a pilgrimage home to Christ. Therefore the most important question of all, the fundamental question at the heart of this book and the reason you are part of it is this: Do you turn to Jesus Christ and accept him as your Savior? Most of the sessions will be about trying to unravel what this means. Who is Christ? What does it mean to be saved? How can I deal with the damaging reality of sin and evil in my own life and in the life of the world around me?

Here are the questions in full. They are worth reading through, not because you are necessarily ready to answer them yet, but so that you know what this part of the *Pilgrim* course is about and you can begin to consider whether you want to follow Christ.

The celebrant asks the following questions of candidates (when they speak for themselves), and of parents and godparents (when they speak on behalf of infants and younger children):

> Do you renounce Satan and all the spiritual forces of wickedness that rebel against God?
> **I renounce them.**

> Do you renounce the evil powers of this world which corrupt and destroy the creatures of God?
> **I renounce them.**

> Do you renounce all sinful desires that draw you from the love of God?
> **I renounce them.**

> Do you turn to Jesus Christ and accept him as your Savior?
> **I do.**

> Do you put your whole trust in his grace and love?
> **I do.**

> Do you promise to follow and obey him as your Lord?
> **I do.**

The second set of questions is directed to the mind, and are about what Christians believe. The whole congregation joins those about to be baptized in answering this set of questions. The Baptismal Covenant is a crucial part of The Episcopal Church's theology and practice. Each query is a real question, and our responses actually matter.

The covenant begins with an interrogatory form of the Apostles' Creed, the historic baptismal creed:

Do you believe in God the Father?
Do you believe in Jesus Christ, the Son of God?
Do you believe in God the Holy Spirit?

The answer to each is a direct statement taken from the Apostles' Creed, with the whole assembly joining in the recitation along with the candidates for baptism, confirmation, and reaffirmation. (The word "creed" just means "belief.") The Apostles' Creed is therefore one of the most ancient summaries of Christian faith—one that encapsulates the belief of the apostles, the very first followers of Jesus.

They capture the very essence of Christian faith which is belief in God as Father, Son, and Holy Spirit. For Christians believe that Jesus is God's Son; that he reveals to us that God is our Father; and that God is available to us through the Holy Spirit.

You won't ever be asked if you understand all this. No one does. But you are asked whether you *believe and trust*. This is called faith. It is a different sort of knowledge. It is the knowledge of being known and loved, and of loving in return. We experience this in human relationships (though we would be hard pushed to prove it). We also experience it in that relationship with God that is the Christian faith.

After these three questions, there are five more questions that work out the implications of Christian faith in one's daily life:

Will you continue in the apostles' teaching and fellowship, in the breaking of bread, and the prayers?

Will you persevere in resisting evil, and, whenever you fall into sin, repent and return to the Lord?

Will you proclaim by word and example the Good News of God in Christ?

Will you seek and serve Christ in all persons, loving your neighbor as yourself?

Will you strive for justice and peace among all people, and respect the dignity of every human being?

The first question asks if they will participate in the sacramental life of the church. The Christian faith is lived corporately, as a part of a worshiping community. There is no such thing as a "private" religion in the life of the baptized. The next question asks if the candidates will persist in resisting evil and repent when they sin. We are humans, so the question is not if we will sin, but what we do when we sin. Another question asks if we will proclaim our belief in Jesus in word and action. This underscores the duty of the baptized to tell what he or she has seen and heard, and it also makes the point that actions tend to speak louder than words.

Finally, two questions squarely address the social implications of baptism. The fourth question demands equitable treatment of others one encounters in one's life. The fifth points toward the need for Christians to combat systemic injustice, and it underscores that the love of neighbor is not restricted to other members of the Christian household: one is to respect the dignity of every human being.

The answer to each of these five questions is a resounding: **I will, with God's help**. Baptism is about discipleship, knowing that God is with us all the way. We are not alone in taking on this serious obligation of Christian practice. God is always helping us along the way.

So, having turned to Christ, you are asked if you believe and trust in the God who Jesus reveals to be personal and communal; a God of infinite loving relationship; a God with whom you are invited to enjoy relationship here on earth and for eternity. Over these seven sessions all this will be celebrated and explored in the hope that you will be able to make this decision yourself one day.

DO YOU TURN TO JESUS CHRIST?

pilgrim

In this session we look at the attraction and the attractiveness of Jesus Christ. We start with a story about people finding Jesus and spending time with him.

Opening Prayers

Lord, lead me on the way of faith:
help me to follow Christ.

Open my heart to receive your love,
open my mind to understand your word.

Gladden the soul of your servant,
for to you, O LORD, I lift up my soul.

For you, LORD, are good and forgiving,
and great is your love toward all who call upon you.

Teach me your way, O LORD, and I will walk in your truth;
knit my heart to you that I may fear your Name.

I will thank you, O LORD my God, with all my heart,
and glorify your Name for evermore.

PSALM 86:4-5, 11-12

Now that we have been put right with God through faith,
we have peace with God through our Lord Jesus Christ.
He has brought us by faith into the grace of God.
We rejoice in the hope of sharing God's glory.
This hope does not deceive us:
God has poured his love into our hearts by the gift of his Spirit.

BASED ON ROMANS 5:1-2, 5

Loving God, open my eyes to see Jesus
and to know his purpose for my life.
Amen.

Conversation

What made you come to this course? Share something that has prompted you to want to find out more about the Christian faith.

Reflecting on Scripture

Reading

The next day John again was standing with two of his disciples, [36]and as he watched Jesus walk by, he exclaimed, "Look, here is the Lamb of God!" [37]The two disciples heard him say this, and they followed Jesus. [38]When Jesus turned and saw them following, he said to them, "What are you looking for?" They said to him, "Rabbi" (which translated means Teacher), "where are you staying?" [39]He said to them, "Come and see." They came and saw where he was staying, and they remained with him that day. It was about four o'clock in the afternoon. [40]One of the two who heard John speak and followed him was Andrew, Simon Peter's brother. [41]He first found his brother Simon and said to him, "We have found the Messiah" (which is translated Anointed). [42]He brought Simon to Jesus, who looked at him and said, "You are Simon son of John. You are to be called Cephas" (which is translated Peter).

JOHN 1:35-42

Explanatory note

The word *Messiah* is, as the passage says, the Hebrew for "anointed." In Greek this word is *Christ*.

The *John* referred to in the passage is John the Baptist (or baptizer), a prophet and contemporary of Jesus. We will look at his role in more detail in Session Two.

● Read the passage through once.

● Keep a few moments' silence.

● Read the passage a second time with different voices.

● Invite everyone to say aloud a word or phrase that strikes them.

● Read the passage a third time.

● Share together what this word or phrase might mean and what questions it raises.

"Who are you looking for?"

There's a clue in the title of this session. The Christian faith is all about Jesus Christ. Without Jesus there is no Christianity.

Jesus was a real person. We know of his life, his death, and its impact from sources outside of the Bible and from archaeological evidence.

The question that each of us needs to answer is not "Did Jesus exist?", but "Who is he?" Was he just a brilliantly inspired teacher, preacher, and healer? Or was he, as the Christian faith proclaims, God's Son, born as one of us, come to save us from ourselves?

You wouldn't be reading this at all if you didn't have some sort of inkling that this astonishing claim is actually the world's most precious and important truth. But the truth about Jesus is not a truth that can conclusively be demonstrated in the same way as we could demonstrate that two and two is four and that the sun rises in the east. The truth about Jesus is the truth of a relationship.

To understand the Christian faith, you have to get to know Jesus.

What God has done in Jesus is reveal his purpose to us in the only language we really understand: that is the language of another human life. God in Jesus isn't just teaching us God's way or God's law; he is actually showing us God's love. He is showing us what God is like. And we human beings can only understand love through relationships. That is why God sends a man, not a manifesto: a person, not a statement.

Therefore you can only go so far in understanding the Christian faith by reading about it or talking about it. To understand the Christian faith, you have to get to know Jesus. You have to become a pilgrim in the Christian way.

Talking to other Christians will help enormously. Reading the Bible is indispensable. But we also need to learn to pray and to worship. That's why this course will involve as much praying and reflecting as it will do talking and reading. That's why in the Bible passage we are looking at in this session we find people coming to Jesus, finding out about him by entering into relationship with him.

"What are you looking for?" asks Jesus. This is one of life's most important questions. What do we really want in life? What are our greatest hopes and desires? What do we long for? Those two people spend the whole day with Jesus, talking to him, asking him questions, learning from him. It has such an impact that, on leaving, the first thing they do is to tell others that they have found the Messiah. Andrew then brings his brother to Jesus.

In short

Christian faith is not just about ideas, it is a relationship. Jesus shows us God's love, and we love him in return. Being a Christian is about having a deep relationship with Jesus, spending time with him and listening to him.

For discussion

What is it that attracts you about Jesus and the Christian faith?

What people have brought you to Jesus? That is, whose influence or impact on your life has helped bring you to this point of wanting to explore the Christian faith more deeply?

If you were with Jesus for the day like Andrew was, what would you ask him?

"Look, the Lamb of God"

Right at the beginning of this passage when John sees Jesus he says, "Look, here is the Lamb of God." As we have already noted, at the end Andrew says, "We have found the Messiah." These words and phrases may not mean much at the moment, but they are deeply significant.

When John said that Jesus was the Lamb of God he was saying something profoundly important about who Jesus is. Jesus and all his first followers were Jews, and the event that formed the Jewish people was the Exodus. This was when God saved them from slavery in Egypt. Many plagues and torments were visited upon Pharaoh and the Egyptians, but they wouldn't let Moses and God's people go free.

Eventually God sent an angel of death to kill the firstborn of everyone in Egypt. But God saved the firstborn of the people of Israel, and so that they were marked out as those to be saved God told them to slaughter a lamb and paint its blood on their doors. Then the angel of death would "pass over." This is the origin of the Jewish Passover festival, a festival that Jesus faithfully kept each year. But when John says of Jesus, "He is the Lamb of God," those first listeners would have immediately associated Jesus with the Passover lamb, the one whose blood indicated salvation.

We will explore much more about this as we go through this course and begin to piece together what Christians believe, but for now it is important to note that from the very beginning, the first followers of Jesus and the early Church always understood Jesus to be the one sent by God to bring salvation, not just to the Jewish people, *but to everyone*. He is the Messiah; that is the one anointed and chosen by God to bring God's reign of peace on earth.

> **In short**
>
> The Jews of Jesus' time believed that a Messiah was coming to save them. John identified Jesus as the Passover lamb whose blood brought them salvation, and Andrew said that Jesus was the Messiah. They both believed that Jesus was bringing salvation to the world.

For discussion

- What other questions does this raise for you?
- What don't you understand or where do you need further clarification?
- What might this mean for your life?

Concluding Prayer

Almighty God,
your Son has opened for us
a new and living way into your presence.
Give us new hearts and constant wills
that we may learn of your love
and come to worship you in spirit and in truth;
through Jesus Christ our Lord.
Amen.

Sending Out

During this next week reflect on what you have learned and explored in this session. Think about Jesus and how and why you are attracted to him, and through him to God. What else could you be doing this week to get to know Jesus better?

These readings may help you in your reflections:

When the picture of someone has been painted on wood, but then damaged by the elements, we need the presence of that person whose portrait it was if we are to restore their image. And if this material is not discarded, it is because we value and wish to restore the image painted on it. In the same way, the most holy Son of the Father, being the image of the Father, has come into our midst to renew us who have been made similar to him. He seeks us out when we are lost, pardoning our sins, as Scripture says: "I have come to search out and to save that which was lost."

ATHANASIUS (295–373)

Let your door stand open to receive Christ, unlock your soul to him, offer him a welcome in your mind, and then you will see the riches of simplicity, the treasures of peace, and the joy of grace. Throw wide the gate of your heart, stand before the sun of the everlasting light that shines on everyone. This true light shines on all, but if any close their windows they will deprive themselves of eternal light. If you shut the door of your mind, you shut out Christ. Though he can enter, he does not want to force his way in rudely, or compel us to admit him against our will.

AMBROSE (C. 334–397)

Lord, let me seek you in desiring you:
and desire you in seeking you.
Let me find you by loving you,
and love you in finding you.

ANSELM (1033–1109)

To follow Jesus gives us no intelligible program for a way of life, no goal or ideal to strive after. It is not a cause which human calculation might deem worthy of devotion. At Jesus' call the disciples leave everything that they have—not because they think that they might be doing something worthwhile, but simply for the sake of the call. Otherwise they cannot follow in the steps of Jesus. The disciples burn their boats and go ahead. They are dragged out of their relative security into a life of absolute insecurity. When we are called to follow Christ, we are summoned to an exclusive attachment to his person. The grace of his call bursts all the bonds of legalism. It is a gracious call, a gracious commandment. Christ calls; we are to follow.

DIETRICH BONHOEFFER (1906–1945)

DO YOU BELIEVE AND TRUST IN GOD THE FATHER?

pilgrim

In this session we look at what Christians believe about God. We start with a story from the Old Testament, the record of God's dealings with the world before Jesus, where God is revealed as one who cares and loves—like a father or parent.

Opening Prayers

Lord, lead me on the way of faith:
help me to follow Christ.

Open my heart to receive your love,
open my mind to understand your word.

I love you, O LORD my strength.
O LORD my stronghold, my crag, and my haven.

My God, my rock in whom I put my trust,
my shield, the horn of my salvation, and my refuge;
    you are worthy of praise.

I called upon the LORD in my distress
and cried out to my God for help.

He heard my voice from his heavenly dwelling;
my cry of anguish came to his ears.

PSALM 18:1-2, 6-7

Now that we have been put right with God through faith,
we have peace with God through our Lord Jesus Christ.
He has brought us by faith into the grace of God.
We rejoice in the hope of sharing God's glory.
This hope does not deceive us:
God has poured his love into our hearts by the gift of his Spirit.

BASED ON ROMANS 5:1-2, 5

Generous God, loving Father, in Jesus you are one with us so that we may be one with you. Help me walk the way of pilgrim faith, following the path of Christ.
Amen.

Conversation

What are the qualities you look for in a great parent? Share some of your best experiences of being a parent or of being a child.

Reflecting on Scripture

Reading

When Israel was a child, I loved him, and out of Egypt I called my son. ²The more I called them, the more they went from me; they kept sacrificing to the Baals, and offering incense to idols. ³Yet it was I who taught Ephraim to walk, I took them up in my arms; but they did not know that I healed them. ⁴I led them with cords of human kindness, with bands of love. I was to them like those who lift infants to their cheeks. I bent down to them and fed them.

HOSEA 11:1-4

Explanatory note

Egypt was where the people of God were slaves before Moses led them out across the Red Sea.

The Baals refers to the images worshipped by the Canaanites (the people who lived in the promised land before the people of God). They were images of Baal, the Canaanite God of thunder and fertility.

Ephraim is another name for Israel.

● Read the passage through once.

● Keep a few moments' silence.

● Read the passage a second time with different voices.

● Invite everyone to say aloud a word or phrase that strikes them.

● Read the passage a third time.

● Share together what this word or phrase might mean and what questions it raises.

"I taught them to walk"

When you think about God, what kind of pictures come to mind? An old man with a white beard? A king sitting on a throne? Someone distant and far away?

The Bible uses many different images to talk about God, but one of the most common is that of God as a father. Hosea 11:1-4 is a particularly evocative image of God as a parent teaching a wobbly toddler to walk and then catching them in his arms and holding them next to his cheek. It is a beautiful image full of tenderness and love.

Unlike other ancient religions from this part of the world, God is not always described as a distant, all powerful God. God is also portrayed as a loving, caring God who cherishes and nurtures the people.

God is not a distant tyrant figure.

When we get into the New Testament, this image of God as our loving father has developed even further. In the Old Testament, God is described as "like" a father, not just a distant, powerful king; but in the New Testament Jesus encourages us not just to think of God as like a Father, but to address him as Father (as in the Lord's Prayer: "Our Father...").

Jesus intends us to relate to God, just like he does to a loving Father who cares for us so much he is ready at any moment to sweep us into his arms and hold us against his cheek.

This changes our relationship with God almost entirely. It reminds us that God is not a distant tyrant figure ready to swoop down and punish us whenever we put a foot wrong; but a loving, tender father who aches with love for us as we try to walk with wobbly, hesitant footsteps.

The problem, of course, is that the word "Father" is not a positive one for everyone. We use human imagery of God to help us to understand a bit more about who he is and how we relate to him but, frankly, sometimes this human imagery gets in the way.

If we struggle with our human families, then the thought of a divine family will hardly inspire us. What is important is that you allow yourself to recognize that you are loved with a love that transcends any human experience you might ever have had. What is important is the love not the words we use to describe it.

> **In short**
>
> Although we have strong images of God as an old man sitting on the throne, a very important image of God in the Bible is that of God as a loving, caring and nurturing Father. Whatever our experiences of our own fathers, this reminds us that God loves us with a love stronger than any other we will ever know.

For discussion

Can you remember a time when you felt deeply loved? What did it feel like?

When you hear God described as being a Father, what kind of images come to mind?

Is there anything about this image that you find difficult?

An angry God?

One of the things that most puts people off God is the description of his anger. This is most obvious in the Old Testament, but you do find it in the New Testament as well. If God is really a loving God, how can he be so angry?

The answer seems to be found in that love. The angry God we meet, particularly in the prophets, is angry *because* he loves his people so much. The book of Hosea is a particularly interesting example of this. The story of God's anger is told through the lens of the prophet Hosea, who is deeply and profoundly let down by a woman he loves.

Hosea tells us that God feels just like this. God loves the people and is let down again and again by them. As a result God is angry but expresses that anger in the hope that they will return and love God again. Anyone who has found themselves in that position (and we all are from time to time) must surely sympathize with God's loving anger towards God's people.

There is no easy way round the difficult language of God's anger in the Old Testament. It makes us feel uncomfortable and it should. But it stands as a powerful reminder of God's love for us, a love that knows no end.

In short

People are often put off by descriptions of God's anger in the Bible. If you read carefully, however, you realize that this anger exists because of the depth of God's love for us. Love and anger go hand in hand: the more you love someone the more you care when they let you down. God's anger is a sign of God's love.

For discussion

- Can you think of times when you have been angry because you loved someone so much?

- How did that anger express itself? And how did it become an expression of love?

- How have we let down those we love, and how have they expressed their love and their anger to us in ways that have ultimately helped?

- What does all this tell us about God?

Concluding Prayer

Almighty God,
your Son has opened for us
a new and living way into your presence.
Give us new hearts and constant wills
that we may learn of your love
and come to worship you in spirit and in truth;
through Jesus Christ our Lord.
Amen.

Sending Out

During this next week reflect on what you have learned and explored in this session. Think about your own image of God and the Christian idea of God as parent. Reflect on your own experience of parenthood (or another role you have with someone for whom you care deeply) and what this tells you about God.

These readings may help you in your reflections:

In Jesus Christ, God allows himself to be seen, and in seeing God we come alive. Life is a gift, and the means of life is to be found in God alone; so as we come to share the life of God we are also coming to know God and to enjoy his favor.

IRENAEUS (*C.* 130–*C.* 200)

The Lord showed me a little thing, the size of a hazelnut, on the palm of my hand, round like a ball. I looked at it thoughtfully and wondered, "What is this?" And the answer came, "It is all that is made." I marvelled that it continued to exist and did not suddenly disintegrate; it was so small. And again my mind supplied the answer, "It exists, both now and for ever, because God loves it." In short, everything owes its existence to the love of God. In this "little thing" I saw three truths. The first is that God made it; the second is that God loves it; and the third is that God sustains it. But what he is who is in truth Maker, Keeper, and Lover I cannot tell, for until I am essentially united with him I can never have full rest or real happiness; in other words, until I am so joined to him that there is absolutely nothing between my God and me.

JULIAN OF NORWICH (1373–1417)

The hope that we are traveling towards a destiny, rather than a mere collapse, is linked with the faith that our origins were already purposeful. If we think that our existence is a mere fluke, the result of some wildly improbable mix in some primal soup that threw up the conditions required to sustain life, then our whole human story is a chance bubble; it has no purpose and can be pricked as meaninglessly as it was formed. But if there is a Creator who stands outside the whole cosmic evolutionary process, and yet works his will within it by a wisdom and love that are present in its every tiniest movement, then human life has a purpose.

MARIA BOULDING (1929–2009)

DO YOU BELIEVE IN HIS SON JESUS CHRIST?

pilgrim

In this session we begin to look in more detail at who Jesus actually is; the one who is God's Son and the one who shows solidarity with all humanity; the one who shows us what God is so that we can be one with God ourselves. We start with the story of Jesus' own baptism. He is declared as God's Son. He is the one person who doesn't need to be baptized, but he submits to it just the same.

Opening Prayers

Lord, lead me on the way of faith:
help me to follow Christ.

Open my heart to receive your love,
open my mind to understand your word.

Packs of dogs close me in,
And gangs of evildoers circle around me;
        they pierce my hands and my feet;
        I can count all my bones.

They stare and gloat over me;
        they divide my garments among them;
        they cast lots for my clothing.

Be not far away, O Lord;
        you are my strength; hasten to help me.

PSALM 22:16-19

Now that we have been put right with God through faith,
we have peace with God through our Lord Jesus Christ.
He has brought us by faith into the grace of God.
We rejoice in the hope of sharing God's glory.
This hope does not deceive us:
God has poured his love into our hearts by the gift of his Spirit.

BASED ON ROMANS 5:1-2, 5

Victorious God, in Jesus you share our life on earth so that we may
share your life in glory; and on the cross we see the depths and the
extravagance of your love. Help me to stand under the cross so that
I may understand your love for me.
Amen.

Conversation

Who is Jesus? Write your answer on a postcard, or tweet it in 140 characters. What few words would you use to say who Jesus is?

Reflecting on Scripture

Reading

John the baptizer appeared in the wilderness, proclaiming a baptism of repentance for the forgiveness of sins. ⁵And people from the whole Judean countryside and all the people of Jerusalem were going out to him, and were baptized by him in the river Jordan, confessing their sins. ⁶Now John was clothed with camel's hair, with a leather belt around his waist, and he ate locusts and wild honey. ⁷He proclaimed, "The one who is more powerful than I is coming after me; I am not worthy to stoop down and untie the thong of his sandals. ⁸I have baptized you with water; but he will baptize you with the Holy Spirit."

⁹In those days Jesus came from Nazareth of Galilee and was baptized by John in the Jordan. ¹⁰And just as he was coming up out of the water, he saw the heavens torn apart and the Spirit descending like a dove on him. ¹¹And a voice came from heaven, "You are my Son, the Beloved; with you I am well pleased."

MARK 1:4-11

Explanatory note

Wearing a garment made of camel's hair with a leather belt was a sign of being a prophet (see 2 Kings 1:8).

● Read the passage through once.

● Keep a few moments' silence.

● Read the passage a second time with different voices.

- Invite everyone to say aloud a word or phrase which strikes them.
- Read the passage a third time.
- Share together what this word or phrase might mean and what questions it raises.

Reflection   STEPHEN CONWAY

In Jesus, God is one with us...

Crowds went into the wilderness of Judea outside Jerusalem to listen to a preacher called John. This was risky: the people lived under the occupation of the Romans, and the Jewish religious authorities were determined to sustain the fragile peace with Caesar to protect their worship and identity. Like other great prophets before him, John spoke of the coming of a Messiah, an "Anointed One," the Christ. John told people that they had to be ready. God's kingdom was close at hand.

The Jewish hope for a Messiah often seemed to be about the expectation of a king of the Jews like King David from Israel's heroic past. There was, however, another tradition that said that the Savior would be a suffering servant whose kingly closeness to God the Father would be revealed by his bearing the sorrows of the world.

The birth narratives in the Gospels of Matthew and Luke begin the story of God's involvement in the world God made through his beloved Son. He is born of the Virgin Mary. He looks like her because he takes his humanity from her. His life is shaped by an earthly home at Nazareth. And he is God's Son, the one who "will save his people from their sins."

John baptized people with water for the forgiveness of their sins. He was therefore amazed when Jesus appeared before him and asked for baptism. John recognized Jesus as the Messiah whose sandal he was not worthy to untie. As the "Anointed One," he did not need baptism; but Jesus chose this way of revealing how he would identify himself with all of humanity. We are not up to saving ourselves; but God sent Jesus, so that through him we are freed from the power of sin and reconciled to God.

For discussion

What is it about Jesus that surprised and challenged people?

What is it about Jesus that surprises and challenges you?

...So that we can be one with God

Jesus emerged from obscurity to proclaim that in him God's kingdom had come near. Crowds were drawn to him by the signs and wonders he performed. People were freed from all kinds of sickness and inner prisons. He fed them in the wilderness. In everything he did, Jesus revealed the overflowing abundance of God's love. He was often at odds with the religious establishment because he threatened the status quo and condemned them for using their interpretation of the law of God to exclude the people on the margins who were God's favored little ones. Jesus was particularly criticized for those miracles where the lives of conspicuous sinners were transformed. He told them to go in peace because their sins were forgiven.

This was blasphemy to the priests and scribes who knew that only God could forgive sins. Later, when Jesus was dragged before the High Priest, he was asked whether he was the Son of God. He answered, "I am he." This sealed his fate.

Jesus predicted what would happen, though his friends would not face it even as one of them was about to betray him. One of his closest friends, Peter said that he would never betray Jesus, but when Jesus was arrested he was the first to deny knowing him. Jesus' trial was a mockery. Jesus is largely silent. He has allowed himself to be handed over to death. It is no wonder that since his death he has been heralded as the Lamb of God, the one perfect sacrifice, and depicted in art as a trusting lamb.

He was scourged and crucified between two criminals. It was the cruelest judicial death imaginable, and Jesus was spared nothing. He had prayed that this cup of suffering might be taken away, but the only thing that really mattered to him was to be obedient to his Father's will. Paradoxically, it was the only way to free humanity from being defined by death. God had to share it.

Jesus' dead body was laid in the new tomb of a secret follower. The entry to the tomb was barred by a large stone. Imagine the fear and surprise of Jesus' friend, Mary Magdalene, when she found the stone rolled back and the tomb empty. All she could think about was her grief, now compounded by the theft of the body. Looking into the grave, she is not alert to the life beyond it. A voice calls her name, and at last she recognizes Jesus alive before her, but changed. Just as his friends had disbelieved his predictions of his death, they had also dismissed the prediction of his resurrection on the third day.

Jesus revealed the overflowing abundance of God's love.

The Father had completely vindicated Jesus' obedience and trust and had raised him to life as the beginning of the New Creation. Friends, who were cowering in an upstairs room waiting for their own arrest, encountered Jesus and were transformed by the breath of his Spirit to carry the good news of his death and resurrection to every corner of the known world.

This good news about Jesus has reached us. His relationship with God as Father is a model for our relationship with God. His death and resurrection have made that relationship possible. In Jesus, God has become one with us so that we can be one with God. In another very famous biblical passage we are told that "nothing can separate us from the love of God in Jesus Christ" (Romans 8:39).

For discussion

- What questions do you have concerning the death and resurrection of Jesus?
- As Jesus hung on the cross he said, "Father into your hands I place my Spirit." What do you want to place in God's hands?
- When Jesus was raised from the dead he said to Mary Magdalene, "Who are you looking for?" What or who are you really looking for in life?
- How does Jesus' relationship with God help you in your faith?

Concluding Prayer

Almighty God,
your Son has opened for us
a new and living way into your presence.
Give us new hearts and constant wills
that we may learn of your love
and come to worship you in spirit and in truth;
through Jesus Christ our Lord.
Amen.

Sending Out

During this next week reflect on what you have learned and explored in this session. Perhaps read through the story of Jesus' death and resurrection in one of the gospels. Think about Jesus' offering of himself so that we can have life with God and what this means for your life.

These readings may help you in your reflections:

God sent his Son to save us through persuasion rather than through violence, for there is no violence in God. God sent him to call us rather than to accuse us. He sent him to love us rather than to judge us.
ANONYMOUS (c. 200)

The Father accepts the sacrifice of Christ not because he demands it, still less because he feels some need of it, but in order to carry forward his own purposes for the world. Humanity had to be brought back to life by the humanity of God. We had to be summoned to life by his Son. Let the rest be adored in silence. Nothing can equal the miracle of my salvation. A few drops of blood have set free the entire universe.
GREGORY OF NAZIANZUS (329–389)

When we begin to follow Christ in his character and teaching, we will encounter many who will contradict us, many who will try to forbid us, many who will seek actively to dissuade us. This can even occur among those who are companions of Christ. Remember, the people who tried to prevent the blind man from calling out to Jesus were the same people who walked at Christ's side. Whether, therefore, it is a matter of threats or flattery or prohibitions, if you wish to follow Christ, turn to the cross, endure, bear up, and refuse to give in.
AUGUSTINE (354–430)

Anyone today who wants to ask God questions, or desires some further vision or revelation, is not only acting foolishly but offending God by not fixing his eyes entirely on Christ, and instead wanting something new or something in addition to Christ. To such a person God might give this answer: "This is my beloved Son, with whom I am well pleased; listen to him." I have already told you all things in my Word. Fix your eyes on him alone, because in him I have spoken and revealed all. Moreover, in him you will find more than you ask or desire.
JOHN OF THE CROSS (1542–1591)

DO YOU BELIEVE IN GOD THE HOLY SPIRIT?

pilgrim

In this session we begin to think about the Holy Spirit, especially the way Christians believe the Holy Spirit unites and equips the Church and makes Jesus present today. We start with a very famous story from the Bible, the day of Pentecost itself—an important Christian festival—when the Holy Spirit is given to Jesus' disciples.

Opening Prayers

Lord, lead me on the way of faith:
help me to follow Christ.

Open my heart to receive your love,
open my mind to understand your word.

Create in me a clean heart, O God,
and renew a right spirit within me.

Cast me not away from your presence
and take not your holy Spirit from me.

Give me the joy of your saving help again
and sustain me with your bountiful Spirit;

I shall teach your ways to the wicked,
and sinners shall return to you.

PSALM 51:11-14

Now that we have been put right with God through faith,
we have peace with God through our Lord Jesus Christ.
He has brought us by faith into the grace of God.
We rejoice in the hope of sharing God's glory.
This hope does not deceive us:
God has poured his love into our hearts by the gift of his Spirit.

BASED ON ROMANS 5:1-2, 5

Jesus, I dare to ask this: give me the gift of your Holy Spirit.
May the fruits of your victory over sin and death be seen in my life.
Amen.

Conversation

How and when have you experienced—or glimpsed—the presence of God?

Reflecting on Scripture

Reading

When the day of Pentecost had come, they were all together in one place. ²And suddenly from heaven there came a sound like the rush of a violent wind, and it filled the entire house where they were sitting. ³Divided tongues, as of fire, appeared among them, and a tongue rested on each of them. ⁴All of them were filled with the Holy Spirit and began to speak in other languages, as the Spirit gave them ability.

ACTS 2:1-4

Explanatory note

The day of Pentecost was, alongside Passover and Tabernacles, a major Jewish festival also known as the Feast of Weeks, celebrating the giving of the Law on Mount Sinai.

- Read the passage through once.
- Keep a few moments' silence.
- Read the passage a second time with different voices.
- Invite everyone to say aloud a word or phrase that strikes them.
- Read the passage a third time.
- Share together what this word or phrase might mean and what questions it raises.

Reflection STEPHEN COTTRELL

The gift of the Spirit

When Christians talk about God, they are talking about God as he has been revealed in Jesus. Jesus shows us what God is like. His death and resurrection show that God has united completely with us. Sin and death have been defeated, and we can now have intimacy with God, like a child to a parent. He also assures us of God's presence with us beyond the physical presence of his life and ministry.

In Jesus, the future has broken into the present. At first, after the resurrection, he appears to his friends in a form which is physical—they can touch him and see him—but it is not just the resuscitation of a corpse. He is alive with a new sort of life; the life that is to come.

The Spirit given by Jesus propels, provokes, and steers the Church.

These appearances come to an end. But at the end of Matthew's gospel Jesus makes this promise: "I am with you always" (Matthew 28:20). It is through the Holy Spirit that this promise is fulfilled and we experience the presence of Jesus. That's why the beginning of the book in the Bible called the Acts of the Apostles begins with the story we have just looked at: the coming of the Holy Spirit.

The book of Acts tells the story of the early Church and the first Christians. They do extraordinary things, taking the message of Jesus across the whole of the known world in a remarkably short period of time. What starts out as a Jewish sect centered on Jerusalem, becomes a world-wide faith, reaching even to Rome.

If you start to read some of this fantastic story you will find constant references to the Holy Spirit. Because it is the Spirit of God, the Spirit given by Jesus that propels, provokes, and steers the Church and each individual Christian.

So the Church did not sit down one day and invent a complicated belief like the Holy Trinity (the Christian belief that God is three persons but still one God); this was their experience. Through Jesus they knew God as Father. From Jesus they received the Holy Spirit. And this Spirit guided their way and shaped their lives.

In short

After Jesus' death and resurrection, the Spirit rested upon the disciples at Pentecost. This was the fulfilment of Jesus' promise to be with them always. Through the Spirit which remains with us, we experience the power of God in our lives and in the world.

For discussion

What comes to mind when you hear the words "Holy Spirit"?

Why do you think the Holy Spirit was so important to the first Christians?

How do you experience the presence of God today? Would you think of calling this the Holy Spirit?

The fruit of the Spirit

In his letter to the Church in Galatia, Paul says that we must "live by the Spirit" (Galatians 5:16). He contrasts this with living by the flesh. He doesn't literally mean that the things of the flesh are wrong. He means that there are earthly desires, and he lists them—"fornication, impurity, licentiousness, idolatry, sorcery, enmities, strife, jealousy, anger, quarrels, dissensions, factions, envy, drunkenness, carousing" (Galatians 5:19-21)—that lead us away from God. As we shall see in another session, these are what the Church calls sin. Things we say and do which fall short of the standards of God.

By contrast Paul then lists what he calls the "fruit of the Spirit." These are "love, joy, peace, patience, generosity, faithfulness, gentleness, and self-control" (Galatians 5:22-23).

The image of fruit is significant. It is used in the Bible a lot. A good tree will bear good fruit. The very first psalm begins with these words: "Happy are those who do not follow the advice of the wicked, or take the path that sinners tread...but their delight is in the law of the LORD.... They are like trees planted by streams of water, which yield their fruit in due season" (Psalm 1:1-3). Jesus himself says: "No good tree bears bad fruit, nor again does a bad tree bear good fruit; for each tree is known by its own fruit.... The good person out of the good treasure of the heart produces good" (Luke 6:43-45). Therefore, if we are to lead good, fulfilled, and fruitful lives, we need to be rooted in Jesus Christ. This happens through the Holy Spirit. Then the Holy Spirit of Jesus—his presence with us—enables us to bear good fruit, the sorts of fruit that Paul lists.

This is the constant work of the Holy Spirit: bringing things together for good.

This is the constant work of the Holy Spirit: bringing things together for good. This happens in the lives of individuals and churches, and through them it works for the good of the whole community. God longs for there to be peace and justice in the world. He works to bring that about through his Spirit-filled Church, planted itself in what is good and bearing fruit for the good of all.

In short

If we root ourselves in the Holy Spirit then we will bear the fruit of that in our lives. In the same way if we root ourselves in our own selfish desires then that will bear fruit too. The fruits of the Spirit are not optional extras but the natural product of being deeply influenced by the Spirit of God.

For discussion

- When you are gardening it is obvious that you reap what you sow. Share some other experiences where you have found this to be true.

- What fruit do you think God the Holy Spirit may wish to draw forth from your life?

- How might you begin to pray that the Holy Spirit will come into your life to help you to live God's way?

Concluding Prayer

Almighty God,
your Son has opened for us
a new and living way into your presence.
Give us new hearts and constant wills
that we may learn of your love
and come to worship you in spirit and in truth;
through Jesus Christ our Lord.
Amen.

Sending Out

During this next week reflect on what you have learned and explored in this session. Think about those lists in Galatians 5. What things do you need to turn away from? (We will begin to think about that more specifically in the next couple of sessions.) What is the fruit that you long to see in your own life? Having identified one or two things, try and live them out this week.

Turn your back on some habit or grudge that is not of God. Embrace a way of living that though it may not come naturally, speaks of the Holy Spirit's infinite goodness and loving purposes. You may also like to read the Acts of the Apostles, or as we may re-name it, the Gospel of the Holy Spirit!

These readings may also help you in your reflections:

The Holy Spirit comes with the tenderness of a true friend and protector to save, to heal, to teach, to counsel, to strengthen, to console. The Spirit comes to enlighten the minds of those who are open to receive him; and then, through them, the minds of others too.

CYRIL OF JERUSALEM (C. 315–386)

As when a ray of sunlight touches a polished and shining surface, and the object becomes even more brilliant, so too souls that are enlightened by the Spirit become spiritual themselves and reflect their grace onto others.

BASIL THE GREAT (C. 329–379)

The Holy Spirit carries on the work of the Savior. While he assists the Church in the preaching of the gospel of Jesus Christ, he writes his own gospel in the hearts of the faithful. All the actions, all the moments of the saints make up the gospel of the Holy Spirit. Their holy souls are the paper, their sufferings and their actions are the ink. The Holy Spirit, with his own action for pen, writes a living gospel, but it will not be readable until the day of glory when it will be taken out of the printing press of this life and published.

JEAN-PIERRE DE CAUSSADE (1675–1751)

To live in prayer is to live in the Spirit, and to live in the Spirit is to live in Christ. We engage in the mission of the Holy Spirit by being rather than by doing.

JOHN V. TAYLOR (1914–2001)

DO YOU REPENT OF YOUR SINS?

pilgrim

In this session we look at what the Church calls sin: that in-built tendency to get things wrong and God's great desire to put things right. We start with the story of Jesus calling people to repentance and then calling the very first disciples to follow him.

Opening Prayers

Lord, lead me on the way of faith:
help me to follow Christ.

Open my heart to receive your love,
open my mind to understand your word.

Deliver me from death, O God,
      and my tongue shall sing of your righteousness,
      O God of my salvation.

Open my lips, O Lord,
      and my mouth shall proclaim your praise.

Had you desired it, I would have offered sacrifice,
      but you take no delight in burnt-offerings.

The sacrifice of God is a troubled spirit;
      a broken and contrite heart, O God, you will not despise.

PSALM 51:15-18

Now that we have been put right with God through faith,
we have peace with God through our Lord Jesus Christ.
He has brought us by faith into the grace of God.
We rejoice in the hope of sharing God's glory.
This hope does not deceive us:
God has poured his love into our hearts by the gift of his Spirit.

BASED ON ROMANS 5:1-2, 5

Merciful God, we thank you that we have peace with you and with each
other through the cross of Christ. Turn us from the seductions of sin
and the snares of evil to share your peace and mercy in the world.
Amen.

Conversation

Share a story of when you have been forgiven or when you have had to forgive someone else. How did it feel? What difference did the forgiveness make?

Reflecting on Scripture

Reading

From that time Jesus began to proclaim, "Repent, for the kingdom of heaven has come near."

[18]As he walked by the Sea of Galilee, he saw two brothers, Simon, who is called Peter, and Andrew his brother, casting a net into the lake—for they were fishermen. [19]And he said to them, "Follow me, and I will make you fish for people." [20]Immediately they left their nets and followed him. [21]As he went from there, he saw two other brothers, James son of Zebedee and his brother John, in the boat with their father Zebedee, mending their nets, and he called them. [22]Immediately they left the boat and their father, and followed him.

MATTHEW 4:17-22

● Read the passage through once.

● Keep a few moments' silence.

● Read the passage a second time with different voices.

● Invite everyone to say aloud a word or phrase that strikes them.

● Read the passage a third time.

● Share together what this word or phrase might mean and what questions it raises.

The Christian faith in a single word?

Is it possible to sum up the Christian faith in a single word? If it is, that word might be "forgiveness." The Bible in all its different books, encompassing a huge sweep of history, tells a story of how human beings left to their own devices get things wrong (Adam and Eve disobey God's instructions, Cain kills his brother Abel, and so on) and how in Jesus Christ, God puts things right.

This forgiveness works in two ways. First of all, it is about what happened on the cross. This is the center of the Christian faith. On the cross sins are forgiven.

In Jesus Christ, God puts things right.

The Bible has different images and different stories to tell how this happens, but the simplest is the story of enduring and triumphant love. Jesus understood himself to be the one whose own life was to be sacrificed for the sins of the world. He struggles to come to terms with the enormity of this vocation.

On the night before he dies he pleads with God that there might be another way. But in the end he submits completely to God's will. He becomes the perfect offering that we could never offer ourselves. And because his purpose is to restore that right relationship with God that sin destroys, he goes to the cross forgiving the very soldiers who nail him there (Luke 23:34) and promising the thief beside him that paradise awaits (Luke 23:43).

The resurrection of Jesus is the ultimate sign that that there is now complete reconciliation with God. This reconciliation, this forgiveness, is available to everyone. Therefore Peter, in the very first sermon ever preached, says to people that they must "Repent, and be baptized...so that your sins may be forgiven" (Acts 2:38).

But what if I don't feel much of a sinner? And what if I can't work out how this forgiveness works?

Sin isn't just the big things we do wrong. If it were, many of us might conclude we are doing okay. Sin is just as much what we fail to do: the good things left undone as much as the selfish things we did do. And sometimes all of us lie in bed at night regretting missed opportunities for good or harsh words spoken. We all fall short of our own standards, let alone the standards of God. That is sin.

Sin is just as much what we fail to do.

And, no, you can't reduce God's forgiveness to an easy formula. God comes to us as a person not a statement. We need to know this person and enter into the story of his life. Then we can find ourselves like those first disciples, like those first listeners to the first sermon, faced with a question: are we going to repent of our sins and follow in his way?

In short

The whole story of the Bible is a story of God's forgiveness. This reaches its climax in the death of Jesus on the cross where Jesus forgave those who crucified him and set us all free from sin. As Christians we are called to turn away from all those things— whether big or small—that cut us off from God and from each other and to live in the knowledge that we are forgiven.

For discussion

Remembering those stories of being forgiven and of forgiving others, what does this tell us about the nature and power of forgiveness and the nature of sin?

Share your responses to the story of the cross. How does it make you feel? How and why do you think God forgives?

The reorientation of life

In the Bible the word "repent" could just as accurately be translated "re-orientate." Repentance is more than just saying sorry. Forgiveness is more than just sins being wiped away. It is about a complete new orientation of life. So when Jesus says, "Repent, for the kingdom of heaven has come near" (Matthew 4:17), he doesn't just mean say sorry and be forgiven. He means lead a new life.

God won't force us to respond. We are invited to follow.

He embodies and demonstrates a new way of living and a new humanity. We enter into this new life through the door of repentance, but the offer of a new life is there for us whether we repent or not. In the cross and resurrection, God has done everything that is necessary for us to receive and live the gift of this new life. But God won't force us to respond. Jesus invites us to follow him, to have our lives re-orientated. But he also waits.

It is wonderful to hear how those first brothers rose up and followed. But they could have said no. Others did.

You now stand in the same place. You may not completely understand what it means. You don't necessarily know where it is going to lead. But you have seen something in Jesus that has made you want to come this far. He now asks you to repent: to recognize your own need of God; of God's forgiveness, and of God's way of living life. God's kingdom is near to you. Are you going to follow?

There are different ways of responding. If you have already been baptized or confirmed, then you can affirm these promises again as a way of demonstrating your commitment to follow Christ. If you feel that you are carrying a burden of sin and you want to know God's forgiveness in a more personal way, then you can arrange to see your priest or minister one to one and make a confession of those sins. And if you haven't been baptized or confirmed, then this is the way to make a public confession of faith and to be welcomed into the life of the Church. And what is the Church? Well, it is just men and women like you, following in the way of Jesus.

For discussion

Share with each other where you think you are on the journey into faith. Are you ready to consider taking the step of baptism or confirmation or an affirmation of baptismal faith?

What most holds you back?

Concluding Prayers

Some penitential prayers

The grace of God has dawned upon the world with healing for all. Let us come to him in sorrow for our sins, seeking healing and salvation.

Jesus, friend of sinners, you bring hope in our despair.
Lord, have mercy.
Lord, have mercy.

Jesus, healer of the sick, you give strength in our weakness.
Christ, have mercy.
Christ have mercy.

Lord Jesus, destroyer of evil, you bring life in our dying.
Lord, have mercy.
Lord, have mercy.

May the God of love
bring us back to himself,
forgive us our sins,
and assure us of his eternal love
in Jesus Christ our Lord.
Amen.

Almighty God,
your Son has opened for us
a new and living way into your presence.
Give us new hearts and constant wills
that we may learn of your love
and come to worship you in spirit and in truth;
through Jesus Christ our Lord.
Amen.

Sending Out

During this next week reflect on what you have learned and explored
in this session. Think about the many different ways we can reset the
compass of our lives by "turning around," not just saying sorry for the
things we do wrong, but orientating our life differently.

These readings may help you in your reflections:

> It was said of an old man that when his thoughts said to him,
> "Relax today, and tomorrow repent," he retorted, "No, I am going
> to repent today, and may the will of God be done tomorrow."
> THE SAYINGS OF THE DESERT FATHERS (FOURTH CENTURY)

There is a struggle between my regrets at my evil past and my memories of good joys, and I do not know which side has secured the victory. Alas, Lord, have mercy upon me, wretch that I am. See, I do not hide my wounds. You are the physician, I am the patient. You are merciful, and I need your mercy.

AUGUSTINE (354-430)

When we fall through our weakness or blindness our Lord in his courtesy puts his hand on us, encourages us, and holds on to us. Only then does he will that we should see our wretchedness, and humbly acknowledge it. It is not his intention for us to remain like this, nor that we should go to great lengths in our self-accusation, nor that we should feel too wretched about ourselves. Rather he wants us to look to him. For he stands there apart, waiting for us to come to him in sorrow and grief. He is quick to receive us, for we are his delight and joy, and he our salvation and our life.

JULIAN OF NORWICH (1373-1417)

Just as a judge, when sentencing a criminal functions better when guided by reason, conducting the proceedings with tranquillity, rather than allowing himself to have an emotional or violent response to the case; so too we will correct ourselves better by a quiet persevering repentance than by an irritated, hasty and passionate one.

FRANCIS DE SALES (1571-1622)

You can hide nothing from God. The mask you wear before others will do you no good before him. He wants to see you as you are, he wants to be gracious to you. You do not have to go on lying to yourself and your brothers and sisters, as if you were without sin; you can dare to be a sinner. Thank God for that: he loves the sinner but he hates sin.

DIETRICH BONHOEFFER (1906-1945)

SESSION SIX:
DO YOU RENOUNCE EVIL?

pilgrim

In this session we look at the reality of evil, and how the Christian faith invites us to decide whose side we are on in life and how we are going to set the moral compass of our lives. We start with an ancient story: the very first murder.

Opening Prayers

Lord, lead me on the way of faith:
help me to follow Christ.

Open my heart to receive your love,
open my mind to understand your word.

When I was really going through it, I prayed to the LORD.
He answered my prayer, and set me free.

The LORD is on my side,
I am not afraid of what others can do to me.

With the LORD on my side
I will defeat all my enemies.

It is best to trust the LORD for protection.
Don't put your trust in anyone else.

BASED ON PSALM 118

Now that we have been put right with God through faith,
we have peace with God through our Lord Jesus Christ.
He has brought us by faith into the grace of God.
We rejoice in the hope of sharing God's glory.
This hope does not deceive us:
God has poured his love into our hearts by the gift of his Spirit.

BASED ON ROMANS 5:1-2, 5

God, who refuses to stay in remote purity, but comes looking for us
where we fail, grant us the courage to see your face and, in the light
of your grace, to renounce the evil that destroys and embrace the love
that gives life to all. We ask this in the name of Jesus who came to
where we are and is not surprised by what he found there.
Amen.

What is wrong with the world? Share one example of something that upsets or distresses you about the state of the world today. And then one example of someone you admire who is making a difference.

Reflecting on Scripture

Reading

Now the man knew his wife Eve, and she conceived and bore Cain, saying, "I have produced a man with the help of the Lord." [2]Next she bore his brother Abel. Now Abel was a keeper of sheep, and Cain a tiller of the ground. [3]In the course of time Cain brought to the Lord an offering of the fruit of the ground, [4]and Abel for his part brought of the firstlings of his flock, their fat portions. And the Lord had regard for Abel and his offering, [5]but for Cain and his offering he had no regard. So Cain was very angry, and his countenance fell. [6]The Lord said to Cain, "Why are you angry, and why has your countenance fallen? [7]If you do well, will you not be accepted? And if you do not do well, sin is lurking at the door; its desire is for you, but you must master it."

[8]Cain said to his brother Abel, "Let us go out to the field." And when they were in the field, Cain rose up against his brother Abel and killed him. [9]Then the Lord said to Cain, "Where is your brother Abel?" He said, "I do not know; am I my brother's keeper?" [10]And the Lord said, "What have you done? Listen; your brother's blood is crying out to me from the ground! [11]And now you are cursed from the ground, which has opened its mouth to receive your brother's blood from your hand. [12]When you till the ground, it will no longer yield to you its strength; you will be a fugitive and a wanderer on the earth." [13]Cain said to the Lord, "My punishment is greater than I can bear!"

GENESIS 4:1-13

- Read the passage through once.
- Keep a few moments' silence.
- Read the passage a second time with different voices.
- Invite everyone to say aloud a word or phrase that strikes them.
- Read the passage a third time.
- Share together what this word or phrase might mean and what questions it raises.

Reflection   NICK BAINES

Do you renounce evil?

Well, of course I do! Evil isn't that hard to renounce because it is, after all, er...evil. It's the perfect example of a no-brainer.

But that's where I would be wrong. Evil isn't just the extreme version of slight naughtiness, nor is it a unique category of badness. In popular terms, it is the word we attribute to child killers and those whom the tabloids brand "monsters," but in reality it is the sort of moral choice that leads to behaviors that are destructive. It applies to all of us.

Look at the story of Cain and you will see what I mean. Cain doesn't wake up one day and decide to be a "very bad person." He lets a sense of personal injustice gnaw away at him over a period of time—presumably without addressing his growing anger either within himself or with anyone else. But, how did this happen? And what might this ancient text say to us today?

Envy is destructive of both the jealous person and the object of their envy. Cain is cross about his brother's seriousness in bringing the best of his harvest to God when Cain himself just offers a token. Rather than learn about self-sacrifice, trust and generosity, Cain lets his envy grow into anger. The relationship is broken...and there will be consequences to this breach.

What this illustrates is the brute fact that there is no such thing as "private" spirituality or morality. What an individual thinks and feels and decides and does has a social effect. Other people are necessarily impacted by how any other individual lives. Cain's envy grows into anger and his anger will have some expression...and this expression will change the world for everybody else, starting with those closest to him.

An interesting feature of this—which we will all recognize and relate to—is that what goes on inside Cain becomes evident in his physical body: "his countenance fell." It is said that the eyes are the light of the body—that we can look into one's soul when we look deeply into their eyes and how they hold their body. In other words, there is no hiding from the reality and power of what goes on inside our hearts and minds.

This is an important recognition because there are some people who think we can separate a human being out into separate bits that can be addressed without reference to the other bits: body, mind, and soul. But, as Paul makes clear in his letter to the Christian church at Rome (Romans 12:1-2), a person is made of all three and they are interdependent. Who we are shapes how we live—and vice versa. My love of God will be evidenced not by my prayers, but by my relationships with others.

> **In short**
>
> Evil is not just something extreme that seems all too easy to reject. People are not born "evil." They become evil bit by bit over time, influenced by the way they think and feel, and what we think and feel ultimately does affect what we do.

For discussion

Do you recognize the description of evil given here?

What is it that sometimes makes evil so attractive?

What other emotions, as well as envy, make us act badly?

Do you agree that what we think about affects what we do?

Questions that go to the heart

Earlier in the story (Genesis 3) Adam and Eve mess up. Trust in God is side-lined by a curious form of greed. Yet, when God comes looking for them in the Garden he asks a simple question that faces us, too: "Where are you?" The answer is that humanity was hiding from the eyes of God. In this story God again comes out to where Cain has messed up and again asks a question: "Where is your brother?" Notice how the individual has become the social. God is interested not only in what we do as individuals, but in how they affect everyone else.

Notice how the individual has become the social.

Cain replies to God with a question of his own: "Am I responsible for my brother?" The answer that hangs around this whole episode like a bad smell is: "Yes, you are."

Yet, in this account of how evil begins small and grows, there is mercy. In both Genesis 3 and 4 it is God who takes the initiative and comes looking for God's people. It is God who comes out to where we are— even where the earth itself screams out our bloody guilt. Yes, I am responsible for mastering myself; but, God keeps coming into the place of my failure, offering hope. Even Cain was marked by God's protection as he left God behind and walked off to build his own little world.

Renouncing evil is not merely notional. To renounce evil is to determine to be open with God and one another about the bad stuff inside which ruins life outside. It is to deny destructiveness the last word.

On the road to becoming a Christian this is a vital juncture. Despite our fascination with evil and our many failings, God comes looking for us. In Christ he offers forgiveness and a new way of living. Whose side are you on? The side of Christ, or the side that leads to the misery of evil?

> **In short**
>
> Rejecting evil involves being open to and with God: open to the God who comes and searches for us and open with God about the toxic things we have inside us, which, if unchecked, grow and grow and eventually became evil. We can easily be drawn to evil, but we can also reject it and turn to God.

For discussion

What hope do you think there is for Cain as he goes into exile?

What might we do practically to help each other renounce evil?

How might belonging to a congregation or small group help us to renounce evil and encourage others to live in the light?

If you had one question to ask God in the light of this story, what would it be?

Are you ready to make a decision to follow Christ; and what questions does this session raise?

Concluding Prayer

Almighty God,
your Son has opened for us
a new and living way into your presence.
Give us new hearts and constant wills
that we may learn of your love
and come to worship you in spirit and in truth;
through Jesus Christ our Lord.
Amen.

Sending Out

During the week ahead reflect on those small thoughts or feelings that, left unchecked, might grow into destructive emotions or actions. Make a note of those things that tend towards evil, and note what you might do to renounce them and replace them with God's life-giving generosity.

These readings may help you in your reflections:

As Christians we do not put our faith in empty phrases. We are not carried off by sudden floods of emotion or seduced by smooth and eloquent speeches. On the contrary, we put our faith in words spoken by the power of God, spoken by the Word himself at God's command. It was God's purpose to turn us away from disobedience, not by using force so that we end up reduced to the status of slaves, but rather by addressing our free will with a call to liberty.

HIPPOLYTUS OF ROME (C. 170–C. 236)

God, seeing the world falling into ruin through fear, never stops working to bring it back into being through love, inviting it back by grace, holding it firm by charity, and embracing it with affection.

PETER CHRYSOLOGUS (C. 400–450)

O Lord, penetrate those murky corners
where we hide memories and tendencies
on which we do not care to look,
but which we will not disinter and yield freely up to you,
that you may purify and transmute them:
the persistent buried grudge,
the half-acknowledged enmity
which is still smouldering;
the bitterness of that loss
we have not turned into sacrifice;
the private comfort we cling to;

the secret fear of failure which saps our initiative
and is really inverted pride;
the pessimism which is an insult to your joy, Lord;
we bring all these to you,
and we review them with shame and penitence
in your steadfast light.

EVELYN UNDERHILL (1875–1941)

Evil is philistine, kitsch-ridden, and banal. It has the ludicrous
pomposity of a clown seeking to pass himself off as an emperor. It
defends itself against the complexities of human experience with
a reach-me-down dogma or a cheap slogan… Evil is a kind of
spiritual slumming… The evil, then, are those who are deficient
in the art of living. In the end, evil is indeed all about death—
but about the death of the evildoer as much as that of those he
annihilates.

TERRY EAGLETON (1943–)

WILL YOU, WITH GOD'S HELP?

pilgrim

In this session we look at the five questions that conclude The Baptismal Covenant, each of which we answer, "We will, with God's help." We start with a story from the Acts of the Apostles in which the first Christians were baptized and began to follow the teachings of Jesus Christ in their daily life and practice.

Opening Prayers

Lord, lead me on the way of faith:
help me to follow Christ.

Open my heart to receive your love,
open my mind to understand your word.

Blessed is the LORD!
for he has heard the voice of my prayer.

The LORD is my strength and my shield;
my heart trusts in him, and I have been helped;

Therefore my heart dances for joy,
and in my song will I praise him.

The LORD is the strength of his people,
a safe refuge for his anointed.

Save your people and bless your inheritance;
shepherd them and carry them for ever.   PSALM 28:7-11

Now that we have been put right with God through faith,
we have peace with God through our Lord Jesus Christ.
He has brought us by faith into the grace of God.
We rejoice in the hope of sharing God's glory.
This hope does not deceive us:
God has poured his love into our hearts by the gift of his Spirit.
                                        BASED ON ROMANS 5:1-2, 5

O God, you have taught us to keep all your commandments by loving
you and our neighbor. Strengthen us to trust you in all that we do,
knowing that with your help, we can share the Good News with
confidence. **Amen.**

Conversation

Share a story of when you have had to ask for help in your life. Who did you reach out to, and why did you choose them? What was their response? What difference did their help make?

Reflecting on Scripture

Reading

Now when they heard this, they were cut to the heart and said to Peter and to the other apostles, "Brothers, what should we do?" [38]Peter said to them, "Repent, and be baptized every one of you in the name of Jesus Christ so that your sins may be forgiven; and you will receive the gift of the Holy Spirit. [39]For the promise is for you, for your children, and for all who are far away, everyone whom the Lord our God calls to him." [40]And he testified with many other arguments and exhorted them, saying, "Save yourselves from this corrupt generation." [41]So those who welcomed his message were baptized, and that day about three thousand persons were added. [42]They devoted themselves to the apostles' teaching and fellowship, to the breaking of bread and the prayers.

[43]Awe came upon everyone, because many wonders and signs were being done by the apostles. [44]All who believed were together and had all things in common; [45]they would sell their possessions and goods and distribute the proceeds to all, as any had need. [46]Day by day, as they spent much time together in the temple, they broke bread at home and ate their food with glad and generous hearts, [47]praising God and having the goodwill of all the people. And day by day the Lord added to their number those who were being saved.

ACTS 2:37-47

- Read the passage through once.
- Keep a few moments' silence.
- Read the passage a second time with different voices.
- Invite everyone to say aloud a word or phrase that strikes them.
- Read the passage a third time.
- Share together what this word or phrase might mean and what questions it raises.

Reflection   SHARON ELY PEARSON

Life among the believers

"What shall we do?" That is one of the first questions the many followers of Jesus asked each other following his crucifixion, death, resurrection, and ascension. Jesus was no longer with them. Now what should they do? Return home like nothing happened? Peter responds in what we could describe as a Holy Spirit moment—he calls them to repent of their old ways and be baptized with over three thousand responding dramatically to his call. They are no longer helpless and searching for what to do. Their journey of faith would continue beyond the moment they were baptized. They promised to "persevere in resisting evil," and whenever they fell into sin to "repent and return to the Lord." They turned from their old ways of life toward a new way of being, putting the teachings of Jesus into practice.

It was a new way of being.

This new life meant new practices while living amongst non-believers. With words that eventually would form part of The Episcopal Church's Baptismal Covenant, they began a new life—in spirit as well as in action. They "devoted themselves to the apostles' teaching and fellowship, to the breaking of bread, and the prayers." All of these practices were meant to help them continue to grow in the knowledge and love of Jesus Christ so that they might have life in his name while building up the body of Christ (the Church) in a world that was fractured by occupation (the Romans in their case) and disregard for the outcast (the poor, disabled, and "others") from those who had power and privilege. For them it was dangerous to practice this new way, and in time, many would be persecuted and killed for their beliefs.

As time went on in the early church communities that began to spread around the Mediterranean region, baptism was the actual immersion of a

Being a Christian involves body and mind.

person in water (Romans 6:3), preceded by a period of instruction in the Christian faith. The early church used oral instruction—a physical gesture—because it did not have access to written resources. Brett Webb Mitchell writes, "The primary way of learning was through the senses: aural and visual, touch and taste, feeling and movement. Being a Christian was fully an act of the body and mind."

This is what we do when we gather together to study scripture and reflect upon its meaning in our lives. We come together regularly in worship as we experience the Holy amongst us in bread and wine (Holy Eucharist), and consider the implications that has for our behavior in daily life that reflects our faith and belonging to Christ. In baptism, God binds the divine self to us with a covenant promise, and our life in Christ begins. Over and over again in ever maturing ways, we respond by confessing our faith and promising obedience—to follow in the apostles' teaching, fellowship, breaking of bread, and the prayers. We promise to "proclaim by word and example the Good News of God in Christ." Being a disciple means to share the story of Jesus in word and action, which is not always an easy task. While God's promises are forever, our human promises are what we continually strive to achieve. With God's help, we become more perfectly Christ's body in the world.

For discussion

- Which practice of the first Christians are you most comfortable with? Which one gives you the most discomfort? Why?

- Have you ever been persecuted for something you believed in? If so, share a personal story of the circumstance. If not, when have you stood up for something you believed in?

- When do you call upon God for help?

Who is my neighbor?

Jesus repeatedly used illustrations from daily life to answer questions posed to him. One of his most well known parables is the story of the "Good Samaritan" (Luke 10:25-37), which he told when asked, "Who is my neighbor?" Through this story we learn that a neighbor is one who shows mercy to another, even a stranger or the outcast. While told over two thousand years ago, this story continues to have relevance to us today. Baptism is an invitation to live our lives differently, understanding that all of God's creation is holy and deserves our respect and care.

All of God's creation is holy.

The last two questions of our Baptismal Covenant ask how we will live in relationship with one another. Being a follower of Jesus asks us to promise to "seek and serve Christ in all persons, loving your neighbor as yourself" and to "strive for justice and peace among all people, and respect the dignity of every human being." Living as one who has been baptized, we are called to be that reconciling presence of the Body of Christ in the world to all our neighbors.

We do this by practicing hospitality to the stranger, caring for God's creation, and providing for those in need—"the sick and the suffering, the poor and the oppressed, for the unemployed and the destitute, for prisoners and captives, and for all who remember and care for them" as stated in our Book of Common Prayer (p. 384). Living out our baptism compels us to connect with Christians in unfamiliar settings, cultures, and circumstances in our local communities and beyond. We strive to turn away from those attitudes and activities that may separate us from following Jesus' example to love one another as he loves us. We never know how we might meet Jesus in unexpected ways though our encounters with others who are different from ourselves in appearance, opinion, or cultural belief.

To respect the uniqueness of all persons is a promise to act out in gestures large or small of what it means to abide in God's reign—where all people live in unity with God and each other, and where the human needs of all people are met with equity. The mission of the Church is to restore all people to unity with God and each other in Christ. We do this by prayer and worship, proclaiming the Gospel, and promoting justice, peace, and love.

To restore all people to unity.

We are strengthened to act in reconciling, just, redeeming, caring, and peaceful ways through deeds of love and service. Living with an awareness of the poor, needy, and powerless is following in the footsteps of Jesus. Our daily life and work is the context for our loving and serving God. With God's help we can respond more faithfully in day-to-day living and carry the message of God's reconciling love to others.

> **In short**
>
> As baptized Christians, we continue to strive to live into our baptismal promises of prayer and worship, proclaiming the Gospel, and promoting justice, peace, and love in our daily lives. All this we do, with God's help.

For discussion

- Who provides you with a good example of living out these baptismal promises? How so and why?

- Share an example from your spiritual journey in which God opened up a new way to serve others in your daily life at work, home, or in the community.

Concluding Prayer

O God, you prepared your disciples for the coming of your Spirit through the teaching of your Son Jesus Christ: Make the hearts and minds of your servants ready to receive the blessing of the Holy Spirit, that they may be filled with his presence; through Jesus Christ our Lord.
Amen.

Sending Out

During this next week, reflect on how you live out each of these five questions from the Baptismal Covenant. Think about how you are mindful of living in the footsteps of Jesus with all your senses and actions—in word and deed.

These readings may help you in your reflections:

Jesus Christ is the Word of God spoken to all. As I, too, am one of the all, and as I, too, believing and hoping in his promise, may see myself as one who is addressed by his Word, I am empowered, commissioned, and liberated with heart and hand and voice to bear witness to him as this Word of the love of God.

KARL BARTH (1886-1968)

Laity, in particular have as their primary arena for ministry the institutions and structures of society in which they work, learn, and play on a daily basis.

JEAN M. HALDANE (1926-2010)

What does the Lord require of you but to do justice and to love mercy and to walk humbly with your God?

MICAH 6:8B

Lord, make us instruments of your peace. Where there is hatred, let us sow love, where there is injury, pardon; where there is discord, union; where there is doubt, faith; where there is despair, hope; where there is darkness, light; where there is sadness, joy. Grant that we may not so much seek to be consoled as to console; to be understood as to understand; to be loved as to love. For it is in giving that we receive; it is in pardoning that we are pardoned; and it is in dying that we are born to eternal life.

ATTRIBUTED TO ST. FRANCIS OF ASSISI (D. 1226)

We shall have to repent in this generation, not so much for the evil deeds of the wicked people, but for the appalling silence of the good people.

MARTIN LUTHER KING, JR. (1929–1968)

Christ has no body but yours, no hands but yours, no feet but yours. Yours are the eyes through which Christ's compassion looks out on the world. Yours are the feet with which he is to go about doing good. And yours are the hands with which he is to bless us now.

TERESA OF ÀVILA (1515–1582)

Never doubt that a small group of thoughtful committed citizens can change the world.

MARGARET MEAD (1901–1978)

Baptismal living is the "committed response to live out our baptismal promises within God's Creation so all may be aware that we are in communion with a Living and Sustaining God." It is the fullest expression of a person's commitment to the baptismal promises, including ministries in daily life.

THE RIGHT REVEREND THOMAS C. ELY (1951–)

Love implies reverence for one another. In every person, ourselves included, we see one whom God has created, chosen, loved, forgiven, welcomed and celebrated. We therefore see each person as a complex and beautiful mystery, worthy of all this outpouring of God's gifts… The beauty of this mystery, unique in each person, draws us to one another. It inspires our love, and our love allows us, even if just briefly, to transcend the difference between us.

A. WAYNE SCHWAB (1928–)

NOTES

New Patterns for Worship, London, Church House Publishing, 2002:
Opening responses (all sessions) (from p. 231).
Concluding Prayer (all sessions) (adapted from p. 70).
Session Five, some penitential prayers, first prayer (from pp. 93–4), second prayer (from p. 95).
Session Six, psalm verses (from p. 136).

Session One
Athanasius (295–373), On the Incarnation, 10, 14.
Ambrose (c. 334–397), Commentary on the Psalm 118 (Heb. Ps. 119), 12.
Anselm (1033–1109), Proslogion, I, 54.
Dietrich Bonhoeffer (1906–1945), The Cost of Discipleship; ET R.H. Fuller, London, SCM Press, 1959, p. 49.

Session Two
Irenaeus (c.130–c. 200), Against Heresies, IV, 20, 5.
Julian of Norwich (1373–1417), Revelations of Divine Love, 5.
Maria Boulding (1929–2009), The Coming of God, Norwich, Canterbury Press, 2001.

Session Three
Anonymous (c. 200), Letter to Diognetus, 7.
Gregory of Nazianzus (329–89), Oration 45 "For Easter," 29.
Augustine (354–430), Sermon, 25, 7.
John of the Cross (1542–1591), The Ascent of Mount Carmel, II, 22, 5.

Session Four
Cyril of Jerusalem (c. 315–386), Catechetical Lecture 16, 1.
Basil the Great (c. 329–379), On the Holy Spirit, 9, 22.
Jean-Pierre de Caussade (1675–1751), Abandonment to Divine Providence, I, 5.
John V. Taylor (1914–2001), The Go-Between God, London, SCM Press, 1973, p. 227.

Session Five
Anonymous, The Sayings of the Desert Fathers, fourth century.
Augustine (354–430), Confessions, X.
Dietrich Bonhoeffer (1906–1945), Life Together; ET John W. Doberstein, SCM Press, 1954, p. 86.
Julian of Norwich (1373–1417), Revelations of Divine Love, 79.
Francis de Sales (1571–1622), Introduction to the Devout Life, III, 9.

Session Six
Peter Chrysologus (c. 400–450), Sermon 147.
Terry Eagleton (1943–), On Evil, New Haven, Connecticut, Yale University Press, p. 18.
Hippolytus of Rome (c.170–c. 236), The Refutation of all Heresies, 10, 33.
Evelyn Underhill (1875–1941), "A Prayer for Wholeness."

Session Seven

Brett Webb Mitchell. *Christly Gestures: Learning to Be Members of the Body of Christ* (Grand Rapids: Eerdmans, 2003), 157.

Karl Barth. Final 4 found in *Final Testimonies* (William B. Eerdmans Publishing Company, 1977), 14.

Jean M. Haldane. "What Builds the Laity for Ministry?" in *Ministry in Daily Life: A Guide to Living the Baptismal Covenant*, eds. Linda L. Grenz and J. Fletcher Lowe, Jr. (New York: Episcopal Church Center, 1996), 11.

Martin Luther King, Jr. Letter from a Birmingham Jail (1963).

Thomas C. Ely. "About Baptismal Living and Ministry" paper from the Episcopal Diocese of Vermont (2007), as quoted in *Born of Water, Born of Spirit* by Sheryl A. Kujawa-Holbrook and Fredrica Harris Thompsett (Alban Institute, 2010), 9-10.

A. Wayne Schwab. *When the Members are the Missionaries: An Extraordinary Calling for Ordinary People* (Essex, NY: Mission Press, 2002), 180.

CPSIA information can be obtained
at www.ICGtesting.com
Printed in the USA
BVHW08s1321180918
527840BV00002B/10/P